Railways & Recollections
Michael H. C. Baker

First published in 2017

British Library Cataloguing in Publication Data

A catalogue record for this book is available from the British Library.

ISBN 978 1 85794 495 2

Silver Link Publishing Ltd
The Trundle
Ringstead Road
Great Addington
Kettering
Northants NN14 4BW

Tel/Fax: 01536 330588
email: sales@nostalgiacollection.com
Website: www.nostalgiacollection.com

Printed and bound in the Czech Republic

Contents

All the photographs were taken by the author or are from his collection.

Frontispiece: **WARRINGTON** (8B) shed was situated south of the town beside the West Coast Main Line. In residence are Stanier Class 5s and 8Fs and Ivatt Class 2MT 2-6-0s.

Introduction

I had intended to celebrate my last journey home from RAF West Malling on the evening of 15 January 1958, in a 1st Class compartment. In the event circumstances conspired otherwise – good phrase that – but at least it was in a comfortable 1930s Maunsell corridor, steam-hauled, rather than in one of the ghastly Bulleid 2HAL EMUs, the usual fare. Bulleid had some very odd ideas concerning what passengers would put up with – think of the ludicrous 'Tavern Cars', steel-sided vehicles tarted up to look like mock Tudor taverns, with interiors so gloomy that they had to be completely gutted and replaced within a very few years.

The journey marked the end of my two years of National Service in the RAF. Over the years there have been assertions by all sorts of authorities who ought to know better that 'a dose of National Service' is what 'the youth of today needs'. My experience was that it gave one a profound distrust of authority. I was never a rebel, nor were my contemporary Aircraftsman Typists. Typing was possibly the least exciting job in the whole of the armed forces, for which no one volunteered, but it was where you were likely to finish up if you were competent in English. Geoff, for instance, whom I succeeded as typist to the adjutant at RAF Abingdon, was going on to the London

The HAL EMUs, produced immediately before the Second World War for the newly electrified lines to Gillingham and Maidstone, had sparse, uncomfortable interiors, seemingly finished in undercoat. Their riding qualities also left much to be desired, but they were hardly unique among Southern EMUs in that respect.

School of Economics. Joe Hyam had a BA from Cambridge, but for reasons best known to himself he refused to take a trade test and thus had a plaque on his door at RAF West Malling reading 'Aircraftsman 2nd class J. Hyam BA, Education Clerk', while a very nice lad with a slight Geordie accent who, on being asked what he was going to do on his next 48 hour pass, replied, somewhat hesitantly, 'Going to the Lord Mayor's Ball.'

'How on earth did you get invited to that?' I asked.

After more hesitation, back came the answer. 'My father's the Lord Mayor.'

We had no quarrel with the officers, distant figures basically. By 1958 many of those in administration had been flyers who had survived God knows what horrors between 1939 and 1945. I remember one afternoon the adjutant at Abingdon coming into my office, which I shared with a civilian lady typist, to return a letter that needed correcting. 'You National Servicemen are bloody useless!' he exclaimed. 'The only thing I can say in your favour is that you're worth ten of any regular.'

And that was the problem. There was a culture amongst some airmen and some NCOs – certainly not all – as well as a proportion of admin and maintenance regulars, that work was something to be avoided if at all possible.

However, you probably didn't buy this book, or even thumb through its pages – which I'm sure will convince you to buy it – to be subjected to a diatribe, so let us move on to *trains*! That referred to in the opening paragraph was the only steam-hauled one on the West Malling line that broke the electric multiple unit monopoly. Made up of a three-coach set – as I'm sure you know, the Southern loved organising its carriages into sets and giving them numbers – plus several vans, it started around dawn from London Bridge and worked its way, sedately, dropping off newspapers, parcels and the odd passenger, to the Kent Coast. Having recovered its breath it then, equally sedately, made its way back to the capital, ending its journey at Holborn Viaduct. Motive power was invariably one of the former SE&CR rebuilt 'E1' or 'D1' inside-cylinder 4-4-0s. Handsome and highly efficient, they were still, as we shall later see, at this date being called upon on summer weekends to haul lengthy holiday expresses between London and the Kent Coast.

I went back to what I had been doing

before call-up, at a firm of industrial and architectural photographers, founded back in 1864 in the earliest days of professional photography. Sadly the boss, Louis, had in the meantime died and the firm was losing its way. Colour photography was coming in, and we were not geared up for it. We were still wedded to huge, whole-plate cameras, which involved focussing under a black cloth. The camera had no shutter – we simply removed the lens cap and counted out loud the time exposure. Two years in uniform had given me the opportunity to think about my future. I had nearly become an art student at the age of 16, but had lacked the confidence to jump into a world very different from the structured, sheltered one of a public school. Now I was ready for

'E1' No 31507 approaches Tonbridge with the 7.24am London Bridge to Ramsgate train.

it, and at Easter 1958 I enrolled at Croydon Art College. I kept in touch with the photography world and, indeed, within a few years, after some hesitation, the art world embraced it enthusiastically – think David Bailey, Donovan and the 60s.

Croydon Art College occupied a Victorian house with a wonderful conservatory in a park bordering the railway line between East and South Croydon stations. We were encouraged to find interesting locations to sketch, and what could be more interesting than a railway station? Virtually all passenger traffic was handled by electric multiple units, the one notable exception being the Oxted line, where trains could be heard puffing up and down below our Victorian building and would sometimes distract us – well, me at any rate – from the serious business of drawing naked ladies – and gentlemen, for that matter – in the conservatory. The Oxted line diverged from the Brighton main line at South Croydon and climbed up through Selsdon station, which was also served by electric trains from Elmers End. Being so close to South Croydon, it saw few passengers and would eventually close, but that served my purpose admirably for I could sit there undisturbed drawing it.

When I first knew the Oxted line it was the home of various elderly LB&SCR-built tank engines. All were swept away by two new breeds of Brighton-built successors. First came 23 Fairburn-designed 2-6-4Ts of pure LMS origin (Brighton Works constructed 41 in all), then the BR Standard 2-6-4Ts. These tank engines were most handsome. Twenty-three were regularly employed on Oxted line trains in 1958, 17 of them shedded at Brighton and six at Tunbridge Wells. The very last of them, No 80154, had been completed the previous year, and all were kept in commendably clean condition. However, they sometimes struggled with the heaviest business trains on the steeply graded lines through the North Downs and the Weald, and BR Standard Class 4 4-6-0s would be sent to help out at the beginning of 1959, the very first 4-6-0s to be regularly employed on the line.

In the early 1950s Britain's last 'Atlantics', the LB&SCR 'H2s', were still to be seen on the Oxted line, where they were great favourites with the enginemen, and although time eventually caught up with them, the very last, No 32422 *Beachy Head*, survived until 1958. Another duty with which they were long associated was the Newhaven Boat

The conservatory at Croydon College of Art was threatened with demolition but was rescued by John Betjeman, among others, and carefully removed and re-erected beside the Horniman Museum at Dulwich.

A drawing of Selsdon station done on the Oxted line down platform looking across to the Elmers End platforms. By this date only three trains a day called at the Oxted line platforms, and even these gave up bothering the following year. The Elmers End side closed in 1983, the gas lamps remaining to the end, the very last in the London area.

No 80017 has left Upper Warlingham station with a Victoria train and is approaching Riddlesdown Tunnel. On the other side of the valley can be seen the electrified Purley to Caterham branch.

Train. I can remember vividly my first sight of it. In 1946, having promised Akela and his wife, Baloo, to 'do my duty to God and the King', I was enrolled into the mysteries of a Wolf Cub pack, joining the 67th Croydon, which met at the Endeavour Hall in Norbury Crescent. This backed on to the railway line between Norbury and Thornton Heath stations, and before pack meetings we would watch the trains go by. One evening the magnificent sight of a long line of corridor carriages, bearing the legend 'Continental Express London Newhaven Dieppe and Paris', including several vans and a refreshment car, and hauled by a shiny, malachite green named 'Atlantic', presented itself. This was grander than any electric train, even the all-Pullman 'Brighton Belle'. Although electric locomotives took over this duty,

'Atlantics' still appeared on occasions. *Beachy Head* made its final run on Sunday 13 April 1958 with a replica boat train. There was hope that it might be preserved, but this was not to be.

However, many years later a boiler from a Great Northern 'Atlantic', upon which design the LB&SCR locomotive was based, was discovered, and out of this grew the notion of recreating one of the Brighton engines. Recently at Sheffield Park on the Bluebell Railway I got to inspect this replica, already evocatively impressive, and it is hoped that within three years a Brighton 'Atlantic' will once again be seen in steam. Who could have imagined such a thing back in April 1958?

Although electrification of suburban passenger services had begun before the First World War, freight services were still being worked by steam in 1958. My nearest shed was Norwood Junction, well within cycling distance of home but not regarded with much favour on account of it possessing

No 32424 *Beachy Head* heads past Norbury with its last passenger working on 13 April 1958.

no glamorous named engines. Most of its residents were elderly LB&SCR-built 0-6-0s and 0-6-2Ts, which could be seen out and about shunting the suburban yards at Thornton Heath, Streatham Common and elsewhere. The shed did own some even more boring diesel shunters, though this presumably was not how the operating authorities felt about them, and who for reasons best known to themselves paid scant regard to schoolboys' enthusiasms.

Locomotives from a number of sheds, other than those already mentioned, put in appearances in my part of the world; Redhill, Three Bridges and Horsham, for example, out in the country, were strongholds of steam in an otherwise electrified universe.

A Maunsell 2-6-0, of which there were four varieties, was never far away and worked every type of train from heavy freight to two-coach rural locals and weekend inter-regionals. These maids-of-all-work had originated on the South Eastern Railway and were multiplied by the Southern. Then there was their equivalent from the LB&SCR, the 'K' Class 2-6-0s, while another variation on the 2-6-0 theme was the BR Standard Class 4MT.

While modern 2-6-4Ts had done for the larger pre-Grouping tank engines, one class that seemed virtually indestructible was the 'H' 0-4-4Ts. Originating on the SE&CR in 1904, there were still nearly 50 of them at work in 1958. They could be seen at East Croydon,

'H' 0-4-4T No 31544 leaves Tunbridge Wells West with the 3pm service to Oxted, made up of a two-coach ex-LSWR set.

where they took over Oxted line trains that divided there, but were mostly employed out in the country in Surrey, Sussex and Kent on the many still remaining, non-electrified branch lines, often coupled to equally ancient carriages, mostly of SE&CR origin but including some LSWR and LB&SCR specimens

I have just switched on a vintage movie channel and, by coincidence, found myself watching a James Stewart film of 1958, *Bell, Book and Candle*. James Stewart was incapable of making a bad film, but the consensus of the critics, with which I concurred, was that this was pretty middling. The female lead was Kim Novak, over whom I was always somewhat undecided – not in the same league as the mesmerising Ingrid Bergman or the divine

Marilyn Monroe. During 1958 Marilyn, together with Tony Curtis and Jack Lemmon, was making the Billy Wilder film *Some Like it Hot*, which was released early in 1959. Despite Marilyn apparently driving everyone nuts with her inability to remember her lines, the result was confirmation that she lit up the screen in every scene in which she appeared like no other, and *Some Like it Hot* was quite simply the greatest comedy of all time.

Rather less entertaining, but of equal significance, was the founding of the European Economic Community on 1 January 1958, out of which we British are preparing to slink as I write. Definitely more entertaining was the first broadcast of Leonard Bernstein's Young People's Concerts with the New York Philharmonic

1958 Happenings (1)

January
The European Economic Community is founded
Sputnik 1, launched in October 1957, falls to Earth
The first successful US satellite, Explorer 1, is launched into orbit.

February
Egypt and Syria unite to form the United Arab Republic, and Gamal Nasser becomes first President
A hydrogen bomb is lost in the waters off Georgia, USA
Seven Manchester United footballers are among 21 people killed in Munich air disaster
Pope Pius XII declares St Clare the patron saint of television
Bertrand Russell launches the Campaign for Nuclear Disarmament

March
British and Commonwealth team led by Sir Vivian Fuchs completes first overland crossing of Antarctic, using snowcat caterpillar tractors and dogsled teams
The US Army launches Explorer 3
The Bridge on the River Kwai wins seven awards at the 30th Academy Awards
Nikita Khrushchev becomes Premier of the Soviet Union

April
BBC Radiophonic Workshop is established
In Cuba, Castro's revolutionary army begins attacks on Havana

Orchestra, which made him a household name, a position consolidated by his *West Side Story*, which, many would argue, stands alongside *Some Like it Hot* as the greatest of its genre. American composers, led by George Gershwin, proved in the 20th century to be uniquely able to bestride classical, jazz and popular music, making, incidentally, life for music teachers a great deal easier now that lessons no longer needed to consist of copying from the blackboard 'Lives of the Great Composers'. However, there were certainly exceptions. I attended a school in Croydon, Whitgift Middle, now the Trinity School of John Whitgift, for whom Benjamin Britten specifically wrote choral music to be performed at the Promenade Concerts. Back in the early 1950s I used to travel on the tram from Thornton Heath with a number of other scholarship boys, including one Travers who played the violin with the National Youth Orchestra. Now, as I'm sure you'll agree, violin solos are not something the average 13-year-old goes out of his way to experience, but whenever Travers played at assembly, which he did occasionally, the entire school would sit entranced. Many consider Benjamin Britten the greatest British composer of the 20th century, and I can see why, but I would give top spot to Ralph Vaughan Williams, who died on 26 August 1958 after a lifetime of composing the most beautiful music imaginable

At the beginning of the introduction I was less than fulsome in my praise for the RAF, but something for which I will always be grateful was the music club run by two officers at RAF Abingdon, which opened the world of classical music to me. There was also the C of E chaplain, Wing Commander Rev Stanley Harrison. An imposing figure in his mid-40s, he inspired confidence, always had time to listen to young airmen's problems, and might well have been the bravest man I ever met. He had been awarded the George Cross when, happening to be close by when in 1940 an aircraft that had misjudged its landing crashed and burst into flames, he dashed more than once into the flames to pull clear the crew. We used to have a flight of paratroop training Blackburn Beverley aircraft at Abingdon. Ugly and ungainly, I used to watch them lumbering about the sky and wondered how they managed to stay in the air. Shortly after I was posted away from Abingdon, one didn't, crashed, and once again the chaplain dashed into the midst of the fire, pulling men clear.

Weather-wise, February 1958 was the nastiest month of the year, as it often is, although if you were into snowmen and all that went with them then you were well catered for. On 6 February there occurred the greatest disaster to befall a British football team when the airliner carrying the Manchester United team, returning from a match in Belgrade, after refuelling at Munich Airport failed to take off in the slush on the runway and crashed, killing 21 people including seven of the team.

On 24 March Elvis Presley was called up into the US Army; three days later Nikita Khrushchev became Premier of the Soviet Union, his time in office marking a thawing, although certainly not the end, of the Cold War. Elvis never performed in the UK; Khrushchev did.

Back to the cinema, on 1 August the very last of the original Hanna Barbera 'Tom and Jerry' cartoons, *Tot Watchers*, was released. Fortunately these masterpieces can still be watched on TV, but avoid at all costs the dire, later, pale imitations. While on the subject of children's TV, *Blue Peter* first took to the air waves on 16 October: I bet you thought it was a brainchild of Lord Reith – I certainly did. Although trainspotting never featured to a significant degree, not surprisingly the programme did at one point get involved in the restoration of the Peppercorn-designed 'Pacific' *Blue Peter*.

Shropshire holiday

Holidays had always, although not exclusively, been spent in Shropshire, where Mum had been born and where there seemed to be relations in every other cottage – but not so many in stately homes. Our family had long worked in various capacities on the estate owned by the Bibby family, of Liverpool shipping fame. To get there involved virtually a whole day of train travel, which I bore with great stoicism. Having patronised Southern Electric then London Transport to get to Paddington, we would board a Birkenhead-bound express, which almost invariably was in the charge of a 'King' Class 4-6-0. Virtually before I could distinguish a Brussels sprout from mangle worzel, I had decided that the 'Kings' were the finest things ever on wheels, and nothing in the intervening years has persuaded me otherwise.

The 'King' would be in charge as far as Wolverhampton Low Level, where a man with a long-handled hammer would walk the length of our train, smiting each carriage wheel, while the 'King' took himself off for light refreshment at Stafford Road shed, before returning to London. Then it was on to Shrewsbury in our GWR carriage, probably a Churchward 'Toplight' or a somewhat more modern Collett bow-ender.

Finally came a journey in a Crewe-bound stopping train, which would take us to Hadnall, the next station down the line, where Mum's favourite sister, Aunt Agnes, would be waiting for us with her trusty – not rusty – bicycle, upon which would be mounted all the luggage while we would trot alongside, as she pushed, catching up with the latest news until the cottage was reached.

HADNALL The author, aged 10, with Uncle Frank, in the potato field on Hardwick Farm, Hadnall, Shropshire. I am holding the stick that, with a man at each end, would be placed under a 1cwt sack of potatoes and tossed up on to a cart. In the distance the largest of the farm's three American-built Allis-Chalmers tractors, 'Big Alice', is hauling the potato-digger. The cart carrying the loaded potato sacks was horse-powered; Hardwick was a very modern farm, but there was still a need for horses. However, by 1958 the only ones were hunters, and the tractors were all grey-painted Fergusons. The farm briefly owned a big noisy Field Marshall, which made so much noise that it drowned out the sound of the

It may well have occurred to you, dear reader, that the Shrewsbury to Crewe line was London Midland territory – very perceptive, if I may say so!

All this was the prelude to the holiday itself, which would be spent in the cottage rented from the Bibby estate by Uncle Frank, who was the cowman for Hardwick Farm. There we would partake of a tea of glorious Ellesmere pork pie or Wem sausages.

steam-hauled expresses pounding along on the track behind the farm. Its progress was marked by a series of controlled (at least I assumed they were controlled) explosions, but it didn't last long.

OLD OAK COMMON No 6014 *King Henry VII* accelerates past Old Oak Common with the 2.10pm train from Paddington to Birmingham, Shrewsbury, Chester and Birkenhead. It retains the sloping front to the cab, which in the author's opinion made it the most handsome of all the 'Kings', a relic of the days when it was briefly streamlined in the 1930s. He could be replaced by just about anything with six driving wheels and plenty of steam, ranging through the ranks of Swindon-designed 4-6-0s, 'Castles', 'Stars', 'Counties' and 'Halls', etc, to Collett or Churchward 'Moguls'.

WOLVERHAMPTON In 1958 and for many years afterwards a number of carriages on retiring from passenger duties often got a further extension to their career by being taken into departmental service. Here at Wolverhampton is a former London & North Western corridor coach dating from circa 1920, with distinctive toplights, a feature that GWR coaches of that era also favoured. By that time any item of rolling stock from the once great 'Premier Line' still surviving on BR was worthy of note.

SHREWSBURY The arrival and departure of the 'Cambrian Coast Express' was probably the highlight of the day for Shrewsbury trainspotters, with its chocolate and cream carriages and well-groomed locomotives. The penultimate member of its class, No 7036 *Taunton Castle*, built at Swindon in 1950, has just taken over for the run to Paddington; No 7814 *Fringford Manor* has brought in the train from the Welsh coast.

Above: **SHREWSBURY** There were two sheds at Shrewsbury, or Coleham to be precise: the former LNWR and GWR facilities stood side by side and with a common road connecting with the Hereford main line just south of the station. Pictured here in front of the GWR roundhouse are three nicely cleaned 4-6-0s. On the left is No 1017 *County of Hereford*, which appropriately spent much of its time in charge of North to West expresses between Shrewsbury, Hereford, Newton Abbot and South Wales. It still has its original single chimney. Next is No 4037 *The South Wales Borderers*, another very appropriate locomotive to find in border country – Shrewsbury once received two votes in a contest to establish the capital of Wales. No 4037 began as a 'Star', *Queen Philippa*, in 1910 and was converted to a 'Castle' in 1926, being renamed in 1937. On the right is No 1013 *County of Dorset* (quite a long way from home, namewise, although it spent much of its career based at Shrewsbury), sporting its new double chimney.

Left: **SHREWSBURY** Prominent at the former LNWR shed at Shrewsbury are a Stanier Class 5MT 2-6-0 and two Stanier 5MT 4-6-0s. In the background, far left, is a 'WD' 2-8-0, while part of the 'supporting cast', extreme right, is a 'Patriot' 4-6-0.

SHREWSBURY The 12.15pm stopping train to Crewe pulls out of Shrewsbury and takes the sharp curve on which the overnight West of England mail train came to grief with fatal consequences on 15 October 1907. Uncle Frank remembered being taken to view the horrendous but compelling scene the next morning. The train engine is very dirty 'Princess' 'Pacific' No 46206 *Princess Marie Louise*, piloted by Stanier Class 5MT No 44761. 'Pacifics' often worked stopping trains, filling in between main duties on the West Coast Main Line, and the 4-6-0 would have been attached in order to conveniently get it back to Crewe.

HADNALL Stanier 'Pacific' No 46224 *Princess Alexandra* of Polmadie shed arrives at Hadnall, the penultimate station before Shrewsbury, with a stopping train from Crewe. The immaculate condition of the 'Pacific' indicates that it is running in after overhaul at Crewe Works.

HADNALL By 1958 DMUs were beginning to appear on some workings between Shrewsbury and Crewe. A brand-new Park Royal two-car unit has just left Hadnall forming the 5.45pm service from Shrewsbury and is about to pass under Haston bridge.

1958 Happenings (2)

April *continued*
    First CND protest march from Hyde Park to Aldermaston
    Satellite Sputnik 2 disintegrates in space after several orbits
    King of Belgium opens World's Fair, Expo 58, in Brussels

May
    Actor-singer Paul Robeson sells out two one-man concerts at Carnegie Hall, but is seldom seen in public in the US again
    Military coup in Algeria
    Soviet Union launches Sputnik 3
    Cuban government launches counter-offensive against Castro's rebels
    Real Madrid win European Cup

June
    Charles de Gaulle is brought out of retirement to lead France by decree for six months
    Pizza Hut is founded
    World's last fully rigged sailing ship trading under sail alone, built in 1887, sinks
    Brazil wins football World Cup

July
    Earthquake in Alaska causes landslide and mega-tsunami, with waves reaching 525m (1,722ft)
    First parking meters installed in UK
    Revolution in Iraq – King Faisal killed, and Abdul Qassim assumes power
    5,000 US Marines land in Beirut, Lebanon, to protect pro-Western government there

HASTON BR 'Britannia' 'Pacific' No 70032 *Tennyson* speeds past Haston with a West to North express, next stop Crewe.

Right: **NEAR YORTON** 'Patriot' Class 4-6-0 No 45507 *Royal Tank Corps* speeds between Wem and Yorton with a North to West express. In 1958 most such trains were still composed of pre-nationalisation vehicles and the 'Patriot' is hauling a typical collection of ten ex-LMS and GWR carriages, including a restaurant car. The 'Patriots' were the last survivors of the pre-Stanier LMS era still to be found on top-link passenger duties. The first two were nominally rebuilds of the LNWR 'Claughtons' – they utilised the same boiler as the rebuilt 'Claughtons' – and looked like slightly smaller versions of the original 'Royal Scots'. A few were rebuilt so as to be virtually indistinguishable from the rebuilt 'Royal Scots', but the great majority survived until withdrawal in their original form. None were preserved, but to remedy this a replica is well on the way to completion.

Top left: **YORTON** Another 'Patriot', this time No 45515 *Caernarvon*, on rather more humble duties, is pulling out of Yorton, a station that survives although the station house is now a private dwelling. The train is the 12.15 Shrewsbury to Crewe stopping train composed of four ex-LMS non-corridor carriages and a van.

Top right: **YORTON** Just beyond Yorton a Stanier 8F has charge of a southbound goods train. The loco's design originated in 1935 and, like the 5MT 4-6-0s, was multiplied with such enthusiasm that they could be seen not just all over the LMS system, but also in various parts of Europe and Asia – I came across one in Ankara in 1966 – many being exported during the Second World War. There were 663 at work on BR in 1958.

Left: **BIRKENHEAD WOODSIDE** The GWR main line to Birkenhead terminated at Woodside station, beside the River Mersey, but many Liverpool-bound passengers would alight at the previous station, Rock Ferry, and take a Mersey Railway electric train to their destination. Opened in 1886, the tunnel under the Mersey was the second oldest underground railway in the world, the first being the Metropolitan in London. Electrified in 1903, the original carriages, although built in the UK by Westinghouse, were pure American in design – the bogies were built there by Baldwin. Various additions were made to the fleet until 1936. In this picture the second and fourth vehicles are of the original clerestory roof design. Strictly speaking they are outside our time remit, for all had been replaced in 1956/57, but one of the originals was taken to Derby Works for restoration but was unfortunately destroyed in a fire in 1958. At weekends the old Mersey Railway trains would venture out into the Wirral and I travelled in them several times in 1956 when stationed at RAF West Kirkby. On the flat, straight section beyond Meols, they would get up to speeds unknown on their own patch and would bounce up and down in an alarming, if exciting – depending on the mood of the passengers – manner.

CHESTER GENERAL The Great Western, never one for conforming to the norm, liked to call its principal city stations 'General' rather than 'Central'. This applied at Chester, a station that the GWR actually shared with the LNWR, which presumably had no objection to the title. This picture nicely illustrates the situation, with Churchward 2-6-0 No 5399, which, judging by the pristine state of its smokebox, has just had some TLC, standing beside No 44738, one of the post-war, non-standard Class 5MT 4-6-0s with Caprotti valve gear; meanwhile No 42856, a Hughes/Fowler 'Crab' 2-6-0, arrives with a down express. Chester General was a station where you could board a train for London facing in either direction, depending whether your destination was Paddington or Euston.

1958 Arrivals & Departures

Jools Holland	Musician	24 January
Ellen deGeneres	Actress and comedienne	26 January
Mary Chapin Carpenter	Singer	21 February
Nik Kershaw	Singer	1 March
Miranda Richardson	Actress	3 March
Andy Gibb	Singer	5 March
Rik Mayall	Comedian and actor	7 March
Gary Numan	Singer	8 March
Sharon Stone	Actress	10 March
Linda Robson	Actress	13 March
Holly Hunter	Actress	20 March
Gary Oldman	Actor	21 March
Alec Baldwin	Actor	3 April
Peter Capaldi	Actor	14 April
Andie MacDowell	Actress	21 April
Derek Dick ('Fish')	Singer	25 April
Michelle Pfeiffer	Actress	29 April
Catherine Tate	Comedienne and actress	12 May
Paul Whitehouse	Comedian and actor	17 May
Toyah Willcox	Singer and actress	18 May
Paul Weller	Singer/songwriter	25 May
Jennifer Saunders	Comedienne and actress	6 July
Kevin Bacon	Actor	8 July
Pauline Quirke	Actress	8 July
Fiona Shaw	Actress	10 July
Michael Flatley	Dancer	16 July
Kate Bush	Musician	30 July
Bruce Dickinson	Musician	7 August
Madonna Ciccone (Madonna)	Singer and actress	16 August
Belinda Carlisle	Singer	17 August
Tim Burton	Film director	25 August
Michael Jackson	Singer	29 August
Chris Columbus	Film director	10 September
Siobhan Fahey	Singer	10 September
Andrea Bocelli	Tenor	22 September
Irvine Welsh	Author	27 September
Tim Robbins	Actor	16 October
Simon Le Bon	Singer	27 October
Mary Elizabeth Mastrantonio	Actress	17 November
Jamie Lee Curtis	Actress	22 November
Nick Park	Animator	6 December
Alannah Myles	Singer/songwriter	25 December

Edna Purviance	Actress	(b1895)	11 January
Ernst Heinkel	Aircraft designer and manufacturer	(b1888)	30 January
Christabel Pankhurst	Suffragette	(b 1880)	13 February
Duncan Edwards	Manchester Utd footballer	(b1936)	21 February
Harry Cohn	Film producer	(b1891)	27 February
Mike Todd	Film producer	(b1909)	22 March
W. C. Handy	Blues composer	(b1873)	28 March
Ronald Colman	Actor	(b1891)	19 May
Robert Donat	Actor	(b1905)	9 June
Julia Lennon	Mother of John Lennon	(b1914)	15 July
Harry Warner	Warner Bros studio executive	(b1881)	25 July
Gladys Presley	Mother of Elvis	(b1912)	14 August
Ralph Vaughan Williams	Composer	(b1872)	26 August
Marie Stopes	Birth control pioneer	(b1880)	2 October
Pius XII	Pope	(b1876)	9 October
Tyrone Power	Actor	(b1914)	15 November

Right: **CHESTER GENERAL**
Former LMS Fowler-designed 2P 4-4-0 No 40671 reverses out of the western end of the station. The Chester area had been the last home of the surviving LNWR 'Precursor' and 'George V' 4-4-0s, replaced by the 2P 4-4-0s of Midland origin, which were no superior, but probably less tired; they worked stopping trains on the Whitchurch branch, and along the North Wales coast. A '43xx' GWR-design 2-6-0 can be seen in the distance outside the station.

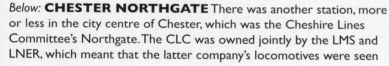

Below: **CHESTER NORTHGATE** There was another station, more or less in the city centre of Chester, which was the Cheshire Lines Committee's Northgate. The CLC was owned jointly by the LMS and LNER, which meant that the latter company's locomotives were seen not only in Cheshire, but across the border at Wrexham in North Wales. Here former Great Central 'C16' 4-4-2T No 67449 stands beneath the station roof, surrounded by carriages of LMS origin. All the 'C14s' were withdrawn by January 1960.

Above: **CHESTER NORTHGATE** The Crosville bus company, which covered a huge area of Wales, Cheshire and Lancashire, regularly parked a choice selection of its vehicles outside Northgate station. Here a splendid Leyland Tiger coach of 1938 leads the parade, followed by Bristol Lodekkas, pre-war Leyland Titans and Bristol single-deckers.

Liverpool and Southport

My first visit to Liverpool was shortly after nationalisation, when some of the old Mersey Railway electric trains were still in their original livery. Later, when stationed at RAF West Kirby, I would ride them at weekends when they would bounce their way along the coast deep into the Wirral. One of the must-do rides on Merseyside was on the Liverpool Overhead Railway. This closed in 1956 and both the last of the old Mersey Railway electric trains and the city's trams were taken out of service in 1957.

On fine summer weekends thousands of day trippers ventured across the Mersey to New Brighton on the last of the steam-powered ferry boats, the *Wallasey*. Built in 1927, she could carry 606 passengers and lasted until 1964, when she sailed across to the breaker's yard at Antwerp. There were 30 million journeys across the Mersey in 1950, and seven million in 1980.

The ferries very nearly ceased altogether at the end of the 20th century, practically all their traffic having been taken by the one railway and the two road tunnels. However, they were still a tourist attraction today, which is not unrelated to the Mersey Beat and Gerry and the Pacemakers' *Ferry 'Cross the Mersey*. Currently there is even a 20-minute commuter service between Seacombe (Wallasey) and the Pier Head, Liverpool, during the rush hour.

LIVERPOOL Many commuters from the Wirral, particularly Birkenhead, Wallasey and New Brighton, used the Mersey ferries rather than the underground trains. Some, as can be seen in this picture, still favoured the bowler hat. In the background three tugs are going about their business, one assisting a freighter bound for Manchester by way of the Ship Canal.

LIVERPOOL was still a prominent passenger port in 1958 with regular transatlantic sailings by Cunard and Canadian Pacific, and Anchor Line to India. Miss Susan Butler is standing in Birkenhead Docks admiring the 1948-vintage, 11,252-ton RMS *Caledonia*, which was employed on the Liverpool to Bombay run, taking 21 days, unless winter storms in the Bay of Biscay delayed her – she once rolled what must have been a terrifying 44 degrees and had to replace every piece of crockery at Gibraltar. For all that she was a popular ship with both passengers and crew; the latter were mostly from Goa, the officers Scots. By the end of 1958 more passengers were travelling across the Atlantic by air than by sea, and the same was happening elsewhere, so the *Caledonia*'s career was cut short, eventually being broken up in Hamburg in 1970. The first jet airline transatlantic passenger flight was carried out by a BOAC Comet on 4 October, to be followed 22 days later by a Pan American Boeing 707. A series of fatal crashes by Comets led to a virtual monopoly by Boeing, which has persisted to the present day.

SEAFORTH Southport, due north of Liverpool and originally served by two terminus stations, was another resort vastly popular with trippers. The Cheshire Lines' Lord Street station closed soon after the Second World War, becoming, rather remarkably, a bus station for a time, but the vastly busier Chapel Street of Lancashire & Yorkshire Railway origin, was served by electric trains from Liverpool and steam ones from Manchester and Preston. One of the 1939-vintage LMS-built EMUs (later Class 502) is leaving Seaforth for Southport.

1958 Happenings (3)

July *continued*
  First life peerage created in UK
  US launches Explorer 4
  Queen Elizabeth II gives Prince Charles
    the title Prince of Wales
  National Aeronautics and Space
    Administration (NASA) established

August
  Last *Tom and Jerry* cartoon made by
    Hanna-Barbera – characters not seen
    again until 1961
  Nuclear-powered submarine USS *Nautilus*
    is first vessel to cross North
    Pole under water
  Nabokov's controversial novel Lolita
    published in USA
  Civil war in China
  US begins nuclear tests over South
    Atlantic
  Notting Hill race riots

September
  First 'Cod War' begins between UK and
    Iceland
  Majority in France vote yes to
    constitution of the Fifth Republic

October
  Guinea declares itself independent from
    France
  BOAC becomes first airline to fly jet
    passenger services across the
    Atlantic, using De Havilland Comets
  Pioneer 1 is first spacecraft launched by
    newly formed NASA

SOUTHPORT This is Southport's imposing Kensington Road station. Very Gothic, it was designed as a passenger station for the West Lancashire Railway by Charles H. Driver and was much admired at the time of its opening in 1882, a worthy portal to a resort that at the time outrivalled Blackpool, just across the Ribble Estuary. However, on the rebuilding of the adjoining Chapel Street station in 1901 by the Lancashire & Yorkshire Railway, which had absorbed the West Lancashire, Kensington Road became redundant. Resuscitated as a goods station in 1913, it served as such until the 1960s. It was demolished in 1982 and a car park now stands on the site. Sad.

SOUTHPORT was once a place of many junctions but, like so many seaside towns, the railway presence has been much reduced. There was a line forming a triangle between the Liverpool and Manchester/Preston routes, which enabled trains such as Grand National specials to avoid entering the station, and was also useful for turning locomotives. Here we see a 'Britannia' 'Pacific' doing just that.

Wales

ABERYSTWYTH Having reached the North West, we can now venture into Wales with a view of Aberystwyth. On the far left BR Standard Class 2MT 2-6-0 No 78000, is setting off, its first carriage a Hawksworth design of the 1940s. Just visible dotted around the yard and the locomotive depot are three 'Manor' 4-6-0s, at that time the mainstay of the principal Cambrian section passenger trains.

ABERYSTWYTH By 1958 the Vale of Rheidol was the only narrow gauge railway owned by British Railways. It was enjoying something of a revival, the locomotives having been painted in lined green livery and the carriages in chocolate and cream two years earlier. 2-6-2Ts Nos 7 *Owain Glyndwr* and 9 *Prince of Wales* are at the heads of trains at the Aberystwyth terminus. These two locomotives were built at Swindon when the GWR took over the line, in 1923/24, to the basic design of the original Davies & Metcalfe predecessors of 1902, but with many typical Swindon modifications. The carriages were also Swindon-built and one can see the resemblance, despite their narrow gauge characteristics, to their main-line counterparts.

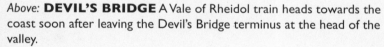

Above: **DEVIL'S BRIDGE** A Vale of Rheidol train heads towards the coast soon after leaving the Devil's Bridge terminus at the head of the valley.

Above right: **AFON WEN** was the junction of the Cambrian coast line to Pwllheli and the former LNWR line from Bangor and Caernarvon. A Stanier 2-6-4T, probably from Bangor depot, can be seen beyond the footbridge on the left.

Right: **TREHERBERT** Still on the subject of Welsh valleys, albeit a very different one, this is Treherbert at the head of the Rhondda Fawr Valley, the last but one station on the former Taff Vale line from Cardiff, 23 miles distant. The architecture is pure 19th-century colliery style, and beyond the station is a slag heap, but steam is in decline, pits are closing, and the train is a newly introduced diesel multiple unit. The line still exists, but the station is much reduced, now just a basic single platform.

GLOUCESTER The Three Choirs Festival, shared by Gloucester, Hereford and Worcester cathedrals, has been a great musical event since the 18th century. In this first picture we see Gloucester shed, very busy with virtually every class of GWR-design locomotive shedded there at one time or another, except for the 'Kings'. It was home to numerous 2-6-0s for some 50 years and here we see the driver of No 5382 making sure his charge is facing the right way. Beyond there are glimpses of a 'WD' 2-8-0, a 'Hall', a '94xx' pannier tank, and a '28xx'.

HEREFORD turning now to Hereford shed, it was shared by former LMS and GWR locomotives. Here one of the long-lived LNWR-built 0-8-0s takes centre stage, with another behind.

WORCESTER was home to several of the highly successful GWR/AEC diesel railcars, which worked over what is now the Severn Valley Railway to Shrewsbury. This is No 11, with, appropriately, a Gloucester RCW body, built in 1936 and withdrawn in 1957. Some of the later railcars were still at work in the area until 1960.

King's Cross

PANCRAS ROAD St Pancras and King's Cross stations sit side by side, divided only by Pancras Road. Heading between the stations past a Renault Dauphine is London Transport Park Royal-bodied AEC trolleybus No 1642, at that time part of the largest fleet of trolleybuses in the world. Behind to the right is King's Cross Hotel, which years later was nearly demolished, but thankfully survived and was instead given a complete makeover. Beyond are a couple of Birch Bros double-deck coaches, and beyond them the celebrated gasworks alongside the Midland tracks on the approach to St Pancras station, featured in many a film. Gasholder No 8 still survives, as a listed structure; it was carefully dismantled, refurbished and restored, and re-erected in 2013, the centrepiece of a line- and canal-side park.

1958 No 1 Records

January
Jerry Lee Lewis   *Great Balls of Fire*
Elvis Presley   *Jailhouse Rock*

February
Michael Holliday   *The Story of my Life*
Perry Como   *Magic Moments*

April
Marvin Rainwater   *Whole Lotta Woman*

May
Connie Francis   *Who's Sorry Now?*

June
Vic Damone   *On the Street Where You Live*

July
Everly Brothers*All I Have to do is Dream/Claudette*

August
Kalin Twins   *When*

September
Connie Francis   *Carolina Moon/Stupid Cupid*

November
Tommy Edwards   *It's All in the Game*
Lord Rockingham's XI   *Hoots Mon*

December
Conway Twitty   *It's Only Make Believe*

KING'S CROSS No 60022 *Mallard*, the world's fastest steam locomotive, departs from King's Cross with the 'Flying Scotsman', arguably the world's most famous train.

BELLE ISLE Accelerating away from King's Cross on its non-stop run to Edinburgh, and approaching Belle Isle signal box with Copenhagen Tunnel beyond, is 'A4' No 60027 *Merlin*. It is about pass under the viaduct carrying the North London line into Broad Street station, over which a London Midland Region, Southern-designed EMU, is passing. Copenhagen Tunnel was the setting for the wonderful 1955 Ealing black comedy *The Ladykillers*.

HOLLOWAY BANK 'A1' 'Pacific' No 60114 *W. P. Allen* pounds up Holloway Bank with a York express, overtaking a BR Standard 9f 2-10-0 on a freight train. An N2 0-6-2T is coupled to a V2 2-6-2. The Peppercorn 'A1s' were excellent machines but never ousted the Gresley 'A3s' and 'A4s' from their London home at King's Cross depot, being concentrated further north. Enthusiasts of the 'A1s' were so incensed that none were preserved that they funded the building of a replica, No 60163 *Tornado*, which on its completion in 2008 captured the headlines and instantly came to rival *Flying Scotsman* in the public's imagination.

HOLLOWAY BANK The bread-and-butter business in and out of King's Cross, the suburban services – which were arguably more profitable than the glamorous, long-distance expresses – was for more than 30 years monopolised by the Gresley-designed 'N2' 0-6-2Ts hauling close-coupled rakes of sparsely furnished, tightly packed, articulated, wooden-bodied 'Quad Art' carriages. No 69543 climbs Holloway bank with a Hertford line train.

Below: **PADDINGTON** departure: one of the British Railways-built 'Castles', No 7022 *Hereford Castle*, is about to have its second express headlamp put in position, then all will be in order for its 8.30am departure for Plymouth and the Royal Duchy of Cornwall. *Hereford Castle* was a Plymouth Laira (83D) resident; Laira 'Kings' and 'Castles' shared 'The Royal Duchy' duties, a train inaugurated in 1956 and still running today.

Above: **PADDINGTON** arrival: No 5094 *Tretower Castle* of 85B Gloucester shed has just pulled in to Platform 8 with an express from Cheltenham and Gloucester, and stands alongside No 5943 *Elmdon Hall* at Platform 7.. Between Platforms 8 and 9 was the taxi road, the vehicles coming down the slope from beside the suburban station, where, uniquely for a London terminus, Underground and suburban steam trains served opposite platform faces.

OLD OAK COMMON No 9707, one of the many varieties of pannier tanks, this one of a group of 11 '57xxs' fitted with condensers for heading through the Metropolitan tunnels to Smithfield meat market, bustles long with an evening goods train from Bishops Road depot, Paddington.

PADDINGTON GREEN I would always make sure to board a 630 trolleybus from the junction of the main Brighton Road and the road across Mitcham Common not later than 9am in order to be at Old Oak Common to view the pride and joy of the Western Region in all its dark green and chocolate and cream pomp thunder past. Alighting by the big bridge spanning the tracks, a couple of stops before the 630's terminus at the most curiously named 'near Willesden Junction', I would cross the road, march down the slope and take up position beside the tracks. There would sometimes be a couple of other spotters there and never once was I challenged by authority.

Several other trolleybus routes also passed close to Old Oak Common, and this is the snow-shrouded Paddington Green terminus of the 662. Behind the trolleybus is a Morris 8; although heavily camouflaged by snow, its distinctive outline is unmistakable.

OLD OAK COMMON A rather grander spectacle, although neither more nor less essential to Western Region business back in the late 1950s, is No 6008 *King James II* accelerating westwards with the 'Cornish Riviera Express'. I always rather hankered after owning a Morris 8 such as the one seen in the earlier picture and on the right here, but had to settle for a succession of Morris Minors.

Right: **OLD OAK COMMON** When *City of Truro* emerged from a long slumber in York Museum to take charge of various enthusiast specials in the late 1950s, it also earned its keep when based at Didcot by working ordinary trains to and from Paddington. Here it poses for its portrait inside Old Oak Common depot.

Below: **TWYFORD** When bad times hit the coal-mining industry between the wars, the Great Western Railway decided to elongate some of its 2-8-0Ts built to handle coal trains in the Welsh Valleys to create 2-8-2Ts, and they proved a very useful adjunct to the '28xx' tender engines. Here No 7239 heads along the Thames Valley near Twyford with a westbound freight.

WOLVERCOT JUNCTION A Churchward 'Mogul' might pop up just about anywhere on the Western Region, certainly until 1960, by which time withdrawals, which had been going on with pauses since the mid-1930s, were really beginning to bite. No 6311, built in 1921 and withdrawn in 1960, has charge of a freight at Wolvercot Junction, near Oxford.

The South West

WEYMOUTH It wasn't until the 1970s that Weymouth station was rebuilt, the goods shed demolished, the station itself modernised and improved – slightly – the track layout revised and most of the sidings removed. Until then, with its semaphore signals, vintage gas lamps and Brunel-designed, much-knocked-about station building, it was a real time-warp.

SALISBURY was an important junction where the LSWR and the GWR met. Western Region 2-8-2T No 7241 is seen arriving at Salisbury with a coal train from South Wales. At this time the Western and Southern had their own separate approaches to the city – the GWR used to have its own station alongside the LSWR one – but nowadays the lines from Bath and the West of England come together at Wilton, some 2 miles to the west of the city.

PLYMOUTH The 'Warship' diesel-hydraulics were based on German technology, the overall design being by Ruari McLean and Design Research Associates, who produced an original and attractive locomotive. They were introduced in 1958 and rapidly began to replace steam in the West of England especially. Here at North Road station, Plymouth, a very new-looking 'Warship' takes on water; it's a pity we don't have a record of the conversation. At the opposite platform is a post-war '94xx' 0-6-0PT, while in the distance is a 'Castle' Class 4-6-0, which may have brought in the Paddington-bound train from Penzance.

BODMIN NORTH The Southern loved to put its carriages into numbered sets, and here one of the later Maunsell two-coach corridor units, typical of the formation of the 'Atlantic Coast Express', stands ready to depart behind 'O2' 0-4-4T No 30236. A 'U' Class 2-6-0 stands in the distance. Although today the 'O2s' are chiefly remembered for their virtual monopoly of Isle of Wight services – the sole survivor lives on the Island – a number still found employment in Devon and Cornwall throughout the 1950s, the last not being withdrawn until 1962.

Southern lines

WADEBRIDGE The London & South Western Railway 'T9s', although not the largest of that company's excellent 4-4-0 classes, were the most long-lived and managed to find employment deep into the Bulleid 'Pacific' era. Indeed, the very last, the now preserved No 30120, was not withdrawn until 1963, the same year that the first of Bulleid's 4-6-2s were taken out of service. No 30718 is seen here on the turntable at Wadebridge in the company of a former SE&CR 'birdcage' brake non-corridor coach, many of which found a niche, after the end of passenger service, in departmental use.

NEW CROSS GATE The very last clerestory-roofed carriages survived on the London Underground right through the 1950s and actually into the 1970s. If you wished to savour the experience of riding in a 1923-vintage veteran, you could not do better than change from your Southern Region EMU at New Cross Gate, as I used regularly to do, and board an East London Line train that would take you through Brunel's Thames Tunnel to Whitechapel and the East End.

SOUTH CROYDON The driver of one of the original Bulleid 4SUBs, the first of which appeared during the Second World War, waits for the right away for London. Nicknamed 'Shebas', on account of being, in the words of King Solomon, 'a very great train,' this was only true in that they could, like the Gresley Quad Arts working out of King's Cross, carry a vast amount of people, in very great discomfort.

REDHILL This view is looking north, and aren't the couple in the foreground the very epitome of a middle class, middle-aged pair of travellers of the late 1950s? They have just alighted from the through Wolverhampton to Margate train, hence the red-and-cream-painted BR Mark 1 carriages, complete with headboards, on the left. There is a wisp of steam from the hidden locomotive, which is about to be replaced as the train reverses here to continue over the virtually straight run through Tonbridge to Ashford and on to its destination.

REDHILL 'U1' No 31901 heads out of Redhill with the 4.18pm train for Tonbridge, consisting of a three-coach BR Mark 1 set.

REIGATE 'S15' 4-6-0 No 30837 crosses the London Road at Reigate, just north of the town centre, with an eastbound freight train. It may well be heading for the yard at Redhill. where it will probably be reformed and continue on to Tonbridge and beyond. The 'S15s' were a Urie LSWR design that was perpetuated and modified by Maunsell, this particular example being of the final 1936 batch. The 'S15s' were the nearest thing the Southern Railway had to a big, modern freight tender engine, although they could also often be seen on passenger duties.

BRIGHTON Despite being in the heart of Southern Electric territory, Brighton depot was home to a wide spectrum of motive power, ranging from Bulleid 'Pacifics' (some built at Brighton), 'Schools' Class 4-4-0s, the last British 'Atlantics', and BR Standard 2-6-4Ts (also built at Brighton) to the extraordinarily long-lived 'Terrier' 0-6-0Ts. Here is the first of the 'Schools', No 30900 *Eton*, immortalised in O gauge by Hornby, and 'M7' 0-4-4T No 30049.

THREE BRIDGES At the shed two 'C2Xs' are prominent, and further off on the left is a 'K' Class 2-6-0.

POLEGATE A stopping train for Brighton composed of two 2BIL units leaves Polegate. A handsome signal box and plenty of semaphores abound. In the immediate foreground the 'Cuckoo' line to Hailsham, Crowborough, Tunbridge Wells and Oxted, soon to be closed, branches to the right, while a goods train, with a distinctive, narrow-bodied Southern Railway guard's van bringing up the rear, occupies the sidings to the left. There was a time when shunting went on at Polegate sidings 24 hours a day.

Right: **BICKLEY**
Former SE&CR
'E1' Class 4-4-0 No
31497 makes a brave
sight as it pounds
through Bickley with
a weekend holiday
express to the Kent
Coast. It's train is
set No 465, nine
Maunsell corridor
carriages, which were
at the end of their
careers, restricted
to such duties and
destined a few
months later for the
scrapyard. Built at
Ashford in 1907, this 'E' Class locomotive,
as it was then classified, was rebuilt and
completely transformed in 1920, while
remaining of fairly lightweight design but
with sufficient power to work the Kent
Coast expresses and boat trains out of
Victoria. So here it is, 51 years later, doing
what it was designed for.

Below: **SEVENOAKS** No 31067, another
of the highly esteemed 'E1' rebuilt
4-4-0s, takes it easy before advancing into
Sevenoaks station with a train composed
of a SE&CR-built three-coach non-corridor
set forming a stopping service to Tonbridge..

TONBRIDGE An 'L' Class 4-4-0 arrives at Tonbridge from the east with a train of four early-1920s-vintage corridors. A variation on the rebuilt 'D1'/'E1s', this was the sort of duty these one-time express passenger engines regularly performed in their later years.

1958 Happenings (4)

October *(continued)*
Blue Peter is first broadcast
Life Peerages Act entitles women to sit in House of Lords
Boris Pasternak wins Nobel Prize for Literature
First transatlantic flight of a Pan-Am Boeing 707
Pope John XXIII appointed Pope following death of Pius XII

November
New UNESCO building is inaugurated in Paris
Bossa nova dance introduced in Rio de Janeiro
French Sudan, Chad, Republic of the Congo and Gabon become autonomous republics within French colonial empire

December
Subscriber Trunk Dialling (STD) inaugurated in UK
Preston Bypass, Britain's first stretch of motorway, is opened
US launches SCORE, world's first communications satellite
Charles de Gaulle elected President of France
Rebel troops under Che Guevara invade Santa Clara, Cuba, and President Batista resigns two days later

TONBRIDGE Rounding the steep curve on the northern approach to Tonbridge is 'King Arthur' 4-6-0 No 30799 *Sir Ironside* with a Kent Coast express. The loco has a small tender, having begun its career on the Brighton section where the runs were short, like the turntables. It is hauling a rake of narrow-bodied, red-and-cream-painted Maunsell corridors that had been designed for the restricted South Eastern main line to Hastings but are finishing their days on other duties.

TONBRIDGE In 1957/58 steam was replaced on the London to Hastings via Tonbridge and Tunbridge Wells line by a fleet of six-car diesel-electric multiple units. Two are seen here at Tonbridge, having arrived from Charing Cross, and are uncoupling so that the front six form an express service on to Hastings, the rear a stopping one. With their flat sides, necessary because of width restrictions in BoPeep Tunnel, St Leonards, and their plain, dark green livery, they were just about the least inspiring-looking trains on the whole BR network. Nicknamed 'Thumpers' on account of their thumping diesel engines, they served their purpose, although they were certainly no more comfortable, and rather less visually appealing, than their predecessors, rakes of Maunsell corridors invariably hauled by a 'Schools', probably the finest 4-4-0s ever built.

Below: **ASHFORD** The SE&CR 'H' Class 0-4-4Ts belonged to a family of pre-Grouping passenger tank locomotives that, despite their relatively small size, proved to be so efficient and adaptable that they often outlasted their successors and were still at work until replaced in the 1960s by the diesels that would wipe out all steam, even the latest BR designs. One thinks in particular of the LSWR, North Eastern Railway and Caledonian 0-4-4Ts, the GNR and Great Eastern Railway 0-6-2Ts, and the amazingly adaptable Great Western pannier tanks. Sixty-six 'Hs' were built between 1904 and 1915, and the last, No 31263, was not withdrawn until 1964. Its final duties were between Three Bridges, East Grinstead and Tunbridge Wells, from whence it passed straight into preservation and today works on the Bluebell Railway. Seen here is No 31521, taking on water at Ashford, where it had been built some 50 years earlier.

Above: **ASHFORD** A high-speed cyclist zooms past the entrance to Ashford Works. The South Eastern Railway opened its works in the town in 1847 and the Southern Railway continued building steam locomotives there until 1944, diesel locomotive construction continuing into early BR days. Later specialising in wagons, the works closed in 1982.

DERBY No 10203, the third of the Southern Region 1Co-Co1 main line diesel-electric locomotives, was built at Ashford in 1954, and is seen here with a highly varied collection of motive power in Derby Works, viewed from the station. Other identifiable locos include No 58114, a 2F 0-6-0, the first of which came out of Derby Works in 1875, and the remains of Midland Compound 4-4-0 No 41143.

FOLKESTONE JUNCTION Prominent is 'Battle of Britain' 'Pacific' No 34084 *253 Squadron*, a highly appropriate locomotive to find at such a location, with the white cliffs in the distance, for it was in the skies over Folkestone and the English Channel that so much of the Battle of Britain was fought in 1940. The actual RAF No 253 Squadron was originally based at Manston, near Ramsgate, before moving to Kenley near Croydon. The other locomotive, standing outside the engine shed, is 'Schools' Class 4-4-0 No 30918 *Hurstpierpoint*. This was the junction for the steeply graded line leading down through the town to Folkestone Harbour station and the cross-Channel ferries. The shed closed in 1961 and the station, latterly known as Folkestone East, in 1965, although there are plans to reopen it. While still intact, the harbour branch is now closed.

Index

Companion volume by the same author:

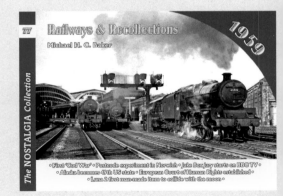